NELL HILL'S

O Christmas Tree

NELL HILL'S

Christmas Tree

MARY CAROL GARRITY

PHOTOGRAPHY BY BOB GREENSPAN

Andrews McMeel
Publishing, LLC
Kansas City • Sydney • London

Nell Hill's O Christmas Tree

Copyright © 2009 by Nell Hill's, Inc.
Photography copyright © 2009 by
Bob Greenspan Photography.

All rights reserved. Printed in China. No part of this book
may be used or reproduced in any manner whatsoever
without written permission except in the case of reprints
in the context of reviews. For information write Andrews
McMeel Publishing, LLC, an Andrews McMeel Universal
company, 1130 Walnut Street, Kansas City, Missouri 64106.

ISBN-13: 978-0-7407-7397-6
ISBN-10: 0-7407-7397-6

09 10 11 12 13 WKT 10 9 8 7 6 5 4 3 2 1

Library of Congress Control Number: 2009923916

Book design by Diane Marsh
Cover design by Julie Barnes

ATTENTION: SCHOOLS AND BUSINESSES
Andrews McMeel books are available at quantity
discounts with bulk purchase for educational, business,
or sales promotional use. For information, please write to:
Special Sales Department, Andrews McMeel Publishing,
LLC, 1130 Walnut Street, Kansas City, Missouri 64106.

Developed by Jean Lowe,
River House Media, Inc., Leawood, Kansas

Photo Stylists: Cheryl Owens
Cecelia Pellettiere
Kelly Acock
Dillon Kinsman
Shana Vaughn

FOR ALL THE CREATIVE PEOPLE
IN MY LIFE WHO SHARE
THEIR TALENTS SO GENEROUSLY
—THANK YOU!

Contents

Tanne   Abies alba

31

Introduction

The Winter Home

One of my favorite pastimes is rummaging through antique stores in the hopes of rediscovering precious items that previous generations treasured and held in high esteem in their homes. On one such recent visit to one of my favorite spots in nearby Weston, Missouri, I discovered a small vintage edition book that was published in German and contained page after page of fabulous line art of trees in all stages of development. And to my complete delight, it was rich with details of pinecones, one of my favorite Christmas decorating tools. The cover of the book was illustrated with a pattern of Christmas trees, reminiscent of the art nouveau movement where artists and designers found their inspiration in nature and brought to us simple decorative designs that reflected that graphic art form.

I have always found my inspiration for decorating in nature, especially at Christmas, when the symbol of this holiday is nothing less than a tree. I also benefit from a host of very talented people who work with me and shop at my stores year-round. Their talents and creative inspiration are especially evident at Christmas, when they begin to help me transform my stores and generously share their personal Christmas customs with me.

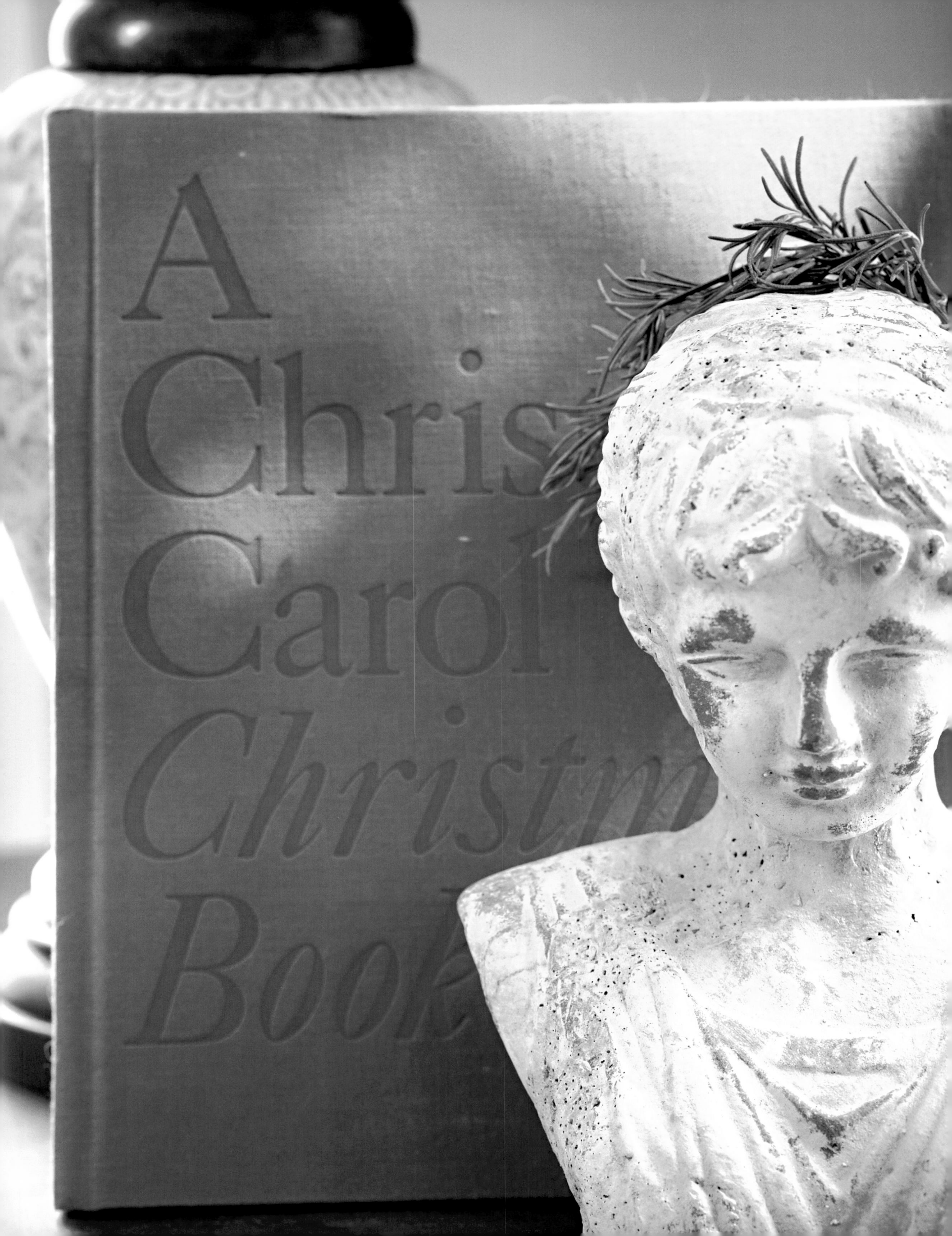
A Chris
Carol
Christm
Book

Our Christmas trees—and the traditions we honor while decorating them—hold tremendous emotional power. Trees connect us to our past while we are reinventing and celebrating the present. A home is truly ready for the arrival of Christmas Day when the tree is placed in the right spot and decorated. It brings us back to the wonder and excitement of our childhood as we reenact our traditions and also reinvent the holiday for new generations.

In my thirty years of going to market to find Christmas ideas for my stores, I have rediscovered Christmas every year with the most popular and recent trends. If you doubt that we are trendy when it comes to Christmas, just recall the aluminum trees with rotating color wheels that were wildly popular forty years ago and are now considered vintage treasures. But for all the color trends that come and go with waves of popularity, the tree remains very personal and is the memory keeper for the whole family.

Everyday objects that we treasure year-round can be elevated to positions of importance in our holiday decor. It can be a single ornament that evokes memories of a young kindergarten child who is now a young woman starting a family of her own. It can be the bunches of broomcorn from your grandfather's farm that you picked in the fall and now tuck into your tree to honor his work. It can be your father's livestock trophy and chaps that claim center stage, or a simple pot of fresh rosemary and a tower of fruit for the cook's kitchen. Even autumn branches that have been captured in silver spray paint and posted at your entrance, with a twinkling ornament to guide visitors, can be the centerpiece of your decor.

One thing I know for certain: Those who shop at my stores tell me that they love books and magazines that let them look inside the homes of others to see what family traditions they are carrying on with their loved ones. In *Nell Hill's O Christmas Tree* I hope I have captured, in photographs and in words, the styles and traditions of creative people whom I have come to know over the years and some new-found friends whose styles I greatly admire and wish to emulate. These imaginative friends have inspired me to new heights of Christmas creativity. Like the original lyrics to "O Christmas Tree," I sing the praises of this wonderful symbol of the holidays and honor the pleasure and glee that its branches bring to us.

I want to wish you a Merry Christmas!

Mary Carol Garrity

PART ONE

All Decked Out

I HONOR
TRADITION
BUT I AM NOT
BOUND BY IT.

Honor Tradition

When I was a little girl, I could not wait until after Thanksgiving, when the family would all pile into the car and go in search of the new holiday decorations and lights that friends, neighbors, and shopkeepers would invent to herald the arrival of this important time of year. The thrill of discovering all over again that spirit of wonder and awe still stays with me today. Customers travel to my stores even earlier than the customary Thanksgiving start (as early as August). Most of Nell Hill's shoppers live more than one hundred miles from my original store in Atchison, and they like to plan trips with their friends before the sometimes harsh Midwestern winters make roads difficult, if not impossible, to negotiate.

But before the winter skies move in, I am already planning what I will do at my home to celebrate this sacred season. Even though I keep my own traditions alive from year to year, like putting my tree in a large garden urn, elevated on a round dining table in my living room, I am always reinventing the holiday.

Anyone who visits my fall open house knows that the five oversized stone urns that connect the posts of the front porch of my large Greek Revival home hold gigantic ferns in the summer and fall. These stone pots are one of my favorite architectural elements of this home and seem to stand guard and define the entrance where the slope of the front yard ends and the entrance to the home begins. In early years, I tried more fanciful and busy natural elements in these urns before settling on a less fussy treatment. My style has evolved, especially in favor of simpler approaches to decorating (that is, simpler for me), although I am all in favor of the big surprise that elicits "oohs" and "aahs," such as hanging artwork or a lantern on the front door.

For this holiday, my front pots hold simple large silver balls nestled in green wreaths that are covered with tiny silver balls. The winter sun's reflection off the glass globes during the day creates a golden sparkle. The soft glow of evening lights reminds me of romantic candles and offers a warm welcome after a full day at the stores.

WARM WELCOME

Before guests even step through the front door at Christmastime, create the kind of warm welcome that makes visitors feel special as they come up the steps. My wide front porch, with terraces on either side, holds visual treats that help establish the mood of the season, such as lanterns with bows and large arrangements of hedge apples or fresh green apples.

This front door echoes the metallic shine of the large silver balls in the porch pots. Place a burnished antique ball on a metal wreath covered with a tuft of moss and simply tuck in berries and fresh greens that are repeated in the urns guarding either side of the entry. As a final statement, suspend a very large pinecone from the center of the base of the wreath. It's simple in form but delivers lots of sparkle when illuminated.

Is there anything more beautifully dressed than Mother Nature herself?

This large black urn on a pedestal announces the transition from my side garden to the stone path that snakes its way around the house. My friends Gloria and Lynda, who are master gardeners, carefully chose the row of emerald green boxwoods, knowing that I would not necessarily be all that careful in their upkeep. However, they did know that the symmetry of the plants would lead the eye both in and out of the little garden.

In the trees that still cling to their leaves well into the start of winter here, hang more green wreaths, suspended by chains and holding pillar candles. In fact, my favorite new invention is the battery-operated candles that allow me to illuminate my outdoor designs without any danger of fire. How far we've come since the days of lighting our Christmas trees with real candles!

On closer inspection, you'll see that the urn contains branches from my autumn yard that have been spray painted copper for a little extra sizzle. Tucked in the foliage, you'll note fresh branches of seeded eucalyptus, fresh evergreens, and large pinecones, called sugar pine cones. These natural jewels of holiday decor are known for their giant size and are harvested from our national forests. I call them "sugar pine cones" because they look so sweet in all my holiday arrangements, you don't need that many to make a sweet statement, and their affordability is a sweet surprise. In fact, if you work with your favorite florist or even find your own direct source, such as boxwoods in your yard that need clipping, greens are an amazing way to dress up your winter yard.

Simple transformations tell the story

As you wind your way to the back of the path toward the stone wall plaque that is centurion of this little side yard, you'll discover my screened porch, which also gets little makeovers for the arrival of winter. The black-and-white striped mattress ticking on the chaise longue gets a small throw pillow in traditional plaid. Move your glass apothecary jars from the dining room sideboard to the screen porch and fill them with nuts that have been spray painted gold and silver (how simple is that?). Mix in green apples on risers for a burst of green; pomegranates or hedge apples could also be used. Birds hold court (I can't do anything without including these winged wonders) alongside a bronze deer. My favorite things look different in the light of winter, and to me that's the fun of it all. We all prize a few special objects for their sentimentality, but at Christmastime we give them center stage, elevate them to levels of importance, and in the process rekindle our own memories of family, special seasonal gifts, and the wonder of nature and the beauty it provides us for all occasions.

Among the precious memories, place one special treasured ornament in a bed of greens and pinecones. This one little detail, among all the others, tells the story that Christmas has arrived.

THAT OLD BLACK MAGIC

I am always amazed to see what my friends Ann and Guy Humphreys create at their ranch-style home in nearby St. Joseph, Missouri. Ann, like me, adores black and white and uses it liberally throughout her home. Christmas gets the same two-tone approach. Her louvered black double front door provides a perfect backdrop for greens that are accented with a crisp black-and-white bow. Following one color scheme—for Ann it was the use of this ribbon—allows you to instantly tie together the decorating plan. A little silver votive hangs in the center of the wreath and adds a pop of silver.

Look closely at the black urn in front of the door and you'll see that a pre-lit garland is wrapped around a rustic metal orb. This arrangement gives her greens more height. The pre-lit garland that wraps the door frame is enhanced with fresh holly.

Ann and Guy's home overlooks a golf course, and these large white lanterns with black lids are used liberally around the outside of the house. This plan is carried around back to the black wrought iron patio furniture, where many lanterns of various sizes are lit up in the winter night, surrounding their various living areas with a soft glow.

OPEN HOUSE

It isn't just front doors that herald the arrival of Christmas. Aimee and Mark Sesler and their three young children welcome the arrival of the holidays by setting the mood at the front gate. Mark is chief marketing officer of Russell Stover candy, so chocolate treats at Christmas are an integral part of the traditions in this busy household. On this particular snowy evening, Aimee is planning to host a holiday party at their home, just a week before the arrival of her large family for Christmas Day.

I encouraged Aimee to use the same ribbon on the gate that would be repeated in her dining room and kitchen decorating plan. The entrance to her home is dressed simply with one very large fresh evergreen wreath. This allows the beauty of the front door, with its beveled glass, to steal the show. Candles are lit in the upstairs windows, and a fresh layer of snow provides an extra wintry punch of wonder.

The family frequently uses the outdoor fireplace, where the hardscape of the stone architecture meets up with the landscape of real holly trees. The urn by the fireplace holds a tray of hot chocolate and oversized marshmallows for roasting—a favorite winter treat for this family.

Wreaths That Wow

Designers at my stores are experts at putting together the wreaths you see here. Our tricks and tips:

To give an old wreath new life, choose a new contrasting garland that can be looped over several times to create fullness at the center of your wreath.

Fishing line, or 26-gauge green wire, is invisible to the eye and allows you to wire many loose ends of the greens together. It also securely holds precious ornaments in place and you can use it to affix loose ends of bows to look like they are entwined in the wreath.

Use a few uniform elements; don't try to do it all on one wreath. One oversized ornament may be all that you need.

Preformed artificial wreaths can be used over and reinvented every season and every year. Use them as the base for adding all kinds of fresh ingredients, such as fruit, flowers, fresh greens, or tufts of moss, for a more natural look.

Wreaths turned on their sides make great greens for centerpieces. They can also be used as natural chandeliers, when they are suspended from ceilings over occasional tables or on porches.

Don't skimp on the bows. Even if you buy only one large spool of ribbon, it will have a big impact. For a different effect, tie the bow in a big knot at the base of the wreath. Or suspend the wreath from the top with an elaborate, loopy bow above the wreath. And make sure the tails of your ribbon are neatly cut. We prefer a "V" cut or a simple angle cut.

Tools to have on hand include wire cutters, florists' wire, a hot glue gun (a necessity for holding small natural elements in place), and fishing line.

PART TWO

Branching Out

Festive Trimmings

Once the outside of my home is dressed in the season's offering, I move on to the front entrance, where I have begun to transform my home for the holidays. Before the dishes from my husband Dan's fabulous Thanksgiving brunch are cleared away, I am

I am never without ideas that can be over the top yet still attainable. For years, I have been using branches in my decorating plans. When Soledad O'Brien invited me to decorate a home for the holidays on NBC's *Weekend Today,* I gladly accepted. The question was, "How do I get my dead tree branches to Florida?" In the end, I found myself running through

I AM ENDLESSLY INSPIRED BY MOTHER NATURE.

planning to transform my home for the big day. This year, I have opted to keep it simple, but to me that doesn't mean unimaginative or boring. I am all about creating drama and surprise in my home decor, and that can be accomplished with everyday materials, as long as the inventive brain is at work, whether it's my brain or those of my coworkers and customers.

the airport at midnight with a giant box of branches trying to find a cab that could hold such a large bounty. To me, these branches were solid gold. My decorating plan for this newly built hospice home for cancer patients' families depended on having these rustic foundation pieces. Branches suspended from the ceiling look dynamic when you attach glass prisms and other embellishments that shine and sparkle.

This year, I was a little more controlled and kept it a bit more manageable. In years past, you could have found a whole tree's worth of branches cascading from my ceilings and woodwork. Not this year. I recently added a new painting to my entryway, along with monogrammed pillows and chairs. I wanted these pieces to do the talking this season. A few years back, when our daughter was married, I hung a mirror so that more people in my jam-packed entryway could see the reflection of them taking their vows. I've left that mirror there since then, both as a reminder of that happy event and because I love the way it reflects light. This year, I let the drama of the branches reaching

to the ceiling set my holiday mood. I tucked in a bird's nest, which is a symbol of good luck for the coming year. Just add some drooping pinecone branches and put a little silver basket with greens on the tabletop. A jar of Dan's favorite pistachio nuts is an added seasonal treat. We often sit down here to catch up on the day's happenings.

In the den off the entryway, I added a punch of tartan plaid with one of my husband's favorite titles, *Poetical Works of Robert Burns*. This colorful traditional pattern makes an instant holiday statement and stands out in this earth-tone room. A bronzed deer holds her own in this booklover's collection.

Every year, when I hold my holiday open house, I try to outdo the year before by lavishly decorating the long banisters that lead from my entryway to my upper level. Several thousand people show up to tour my home each season, and only my downstairs is open to visitors. It's not because I don't want anyone to see my upstairs (which is often the case), but it's more a matter of logistically handling it while I'm also running three retail stores each day.

This year, in the spirit of thrift, I hoped to offer my customers an alternative to the traditional abundant garland treatment. I opted to decorate the corner posts of my staircase in vertical sprays instead of wrapping garland horizontally.

Living with Mother Nature

When I bring an abundance of fresh greens inside my home, I am also inviting sap, needles, and marks on the walls and woodwork for later cleanup. Anyone who visits my home or my stores knows that I can get quite extravagant with natural elements. Through the years—and through trial and error—I have learned some techniques that help minimize the mess. My husband claims that I have put my painters' kids through college with all my redos. Here's what I know and what my crew has taught me through the years.

If you are going to cover your mantel with greens, cut a length of plywood to fit the top of your hearth. This will protect it from damage, and you can glue, nail, or staple the greens in place.

Make sure your tool kit has lots of fishing line available. The line will hold precious glass ornaments in place among the greens and can be hidden easily.

Use a pre-lit garland for the base. Wonderful faux greens are available, and they are well worth the investment. But do tuck in fresh greens all around the garland. Nothing can take the place of the smell of real greens to set the mood of the room.

REIMAGINE
Relocate
RE-CREATE

This is my mantra for the holiday season. The many massive Midwestern ice storms have provided rich fodder for my plans to relocate. In a large earthenware urn in the entryway of a classic renovated town home in the Plaza district of Kansas City, we relocated large pine limbs that fell under the weight of the ice. Not wanting these beauties to go to waste, our design crew re-created this arrangement, placed it on a wooden riser, and gave these reimagined branches center stage at this three-story walk-up.

This lovely home was inspired by historic homes in the area, and its blueprint was carefully and authentically reproduced with modern conveniences by two very talented women entrepreneurs, Katie Gerson and Maggie Fisher. They presented me and the staff with the exciting challenge of designing the home's three floors from top to bottom. In the entry, we chose a paint color called Missouri Bluffs for its rich neutral palette. Across from the branches we placed a very large black bookcase that is a reproduction piece. We left the umbrella stand and wooden dough bowl in place for the holidays but tied a glass pinecone and acorn dusted in glass glitter to the drawer pull.

UNDERSTATED ELEGANCE

In the living room of this charming reproduction period home, we kept the holidays understated, almost as if the home were ready and waiting for the arrival of guests for the Plaza lighting ceremony that is held in the neighborhood on Thanksgiving night. These creamy silk drapes needed to pool just right on either side of the front windows. In between, we placed a ladies' writing desk in the morning sunlight.

Roses in December

The oval-shaped wooden tray on the ottoman holds a bouquet of white roses and a gold holiday ornament to mark this special time of year.

Christmas Card Station

The ladies' desk provides the perfect place to relax over a cup of coffee while the home-owner works on her Christmas card list. We added a little rosemary wreath around the bust

that is holding up the classic Charles Dickens tale *A Christmas Carol*. The cachepot holds an assortment of fresh branches that scents the room with a holiday aroma.

Continuing through the living room, you'll find a wonderful black bookcase. I think every room should have at least one black piece in it. In this case, we tucked a leather-trimmed plaid flask next to an old papier-mâché tin. Special rare books were gathered in one spot, including the classic *Miracle on 34th Street*. This surprise vignette speaks volumes about the time of year.

The mantel greens are tucked under the gold mirror and have only a hint of clear color that complements the room's colors and fabrics. On this fireplace mantel, less is more. It is important to decide which elements of the room you want to speak the loudest. Keeping the fireplace simple lets the mirror shine in this setting.

BE MY GUEST

As guests arrive for the holidays, the feeling of Christmas outside the bedrooms increases at the landing between the second and third floor. It's a surprise to discover that miniature wreaths have been hung in the hallway window and that garlands featuring large pinecones and gold satin ribbons have been hung vertically on the banisters instead of horizontally.

On the guestroom door, a swag of faux evergreens loops around the doorknob, with pinecone artwork signaling both the season and the invitation into this special guestroom.

As they glimpse inside this decidedly masculine room, a burst of Christmas

greets guests with the garland that is wrapped around the footboard

of the pewter-finished guest bed. The mix of magnolia is wound together

with fresh seeded eucalyptus and pine and is gathered in the center with a

LARGER SPRAY OF GREENS. MAGNOLIA IS ESPECIALLY SUITED TO THIS SETTING, SINCE

ITS GOLDEN BROWN UNDERSIDE AGES BEAUTIFULLY AND WILL ONLY ENHANCE THE

COLOR PALETTE OVER TIME. A SMALL GOLDEN BOW HANGS FROM THE CENTER OF THE

GARLAND. THIS IS ALL HELD IN PLACE WITH INVISIBLE FISHING LINE.

On the animal print chair in the corner, gifts await the holiday traveler, along with milk and cookies. I have always enjoyed leaving little gifts in the guestroom that I have made up for my houseguests. They can be tucked into stockings hung on the bedpost as well. They might be chocolates from a local confectioner or a fresh aromatic candle.

The desk is dressed up in holiday finery as well. The welcome is extended with the addition of a fox-and-hound demitasse set, a vintage set from Royal Doulton. Guests feel special when you have their favorite treats on hand; it's a pretty safe bet to go with chocolates and fine nuts. Throw in a high-quality coffee bean or a special bottle of brandy, and you are sure to hit the right notes.

I AM IN FAVOR
OF UNIFORMITY
IN THEME,
WITH SURPRISES
TUCKED IN.

TUCKED IN COMFORT

Just down the hall from this stylish retreat, at the opposite end of the second floor, the master bedroom suite repeats the style of the garland on the fireplace, unifying both rooms. So often we try to do all things with our holiday decorating, and we miss the mark not because we didn't try but sometimes because we try too hard. I favor uniformity in theme, with surprises tucked in. In the master suite, this beautiful little fresh garland enshrines the bedpost, and a bowl of beautiful pears on the dresser invites morning snacks. The master bathroom, with its soothing winter whites, is punctuated by the addition of fresh pine branches over the soaking tub. The pine provides a subtle and sooth-ing aroma to the steaming bath.

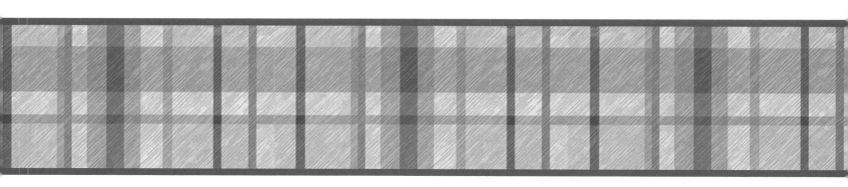

Holiday Retreat

CYNTHIA HOENIG IS ONE OF THE MOST STYLISH WOMEN I KNOW. SHE

AND HER HUSBAND, TOM, BOUGHT THIS CLASSIC BUNGALOW RIGHT

AROUND THE CORNER FROM ME AND REDECORATED ITS SMALL INTERIOR

AS THEIR GETAWAY. I WAS DELIGHTED TO HELP CYNTHIA WITH THE

TRANSFORMATION AND LEARN FROM A REAL ANTIQUE AFICIONADO.

CYNTHIA IS MY CREATIVE DIRECTOR AND VISUAL DISPLAY DESIGNER FOR

MY NEW STORE, NELL HILL'S IN KANSAS CITY.

This small cottage was built by the same era of craftsmen who built my large home on the bluffs of our little town of Atchison, Kansas. Even though this street sprung up a little later than my home, and the home of Amelia Earhart just a few blocks away, it still reflects the grand craftsmanship of the railroad barons' homes of the 1800s and 1900s.

Cynthia and Tom wanted to make this little diamond in the rough their cozy retreat where they could welcome their grown children when they visited for the holidays. As you enter the front door, you are immediately impressed with

the staircase and small alcove window that displays one of Cynthia's favorite pieces: a blue holy water fountain that she discovered at an antiques store. We tucked some fresh greens and berries into this prized ornament and hung it from a moss green silk ribbon. We kept the black banister rail of the staircase visible by loosely draping fresh Noble fir greens mixed with fresh cypress from bottom to top. Wiring was not needed to hold it in place, and the aroma of fresh pine greets visitors at the entrance. This burst of greenery will substitute for a tree downstairs (surprises await us later upstairs!) in this small twelve-hundred-square-foot cottage.

*Happy, happy Christmas, that
can win us back to the delusions
of our childhood days, recall
to the old man the pleasures
of his youth, and transport
the traveler back to his own
fireside and quiet home!*

—CHARLES DICKENS

VISIONS OF SUGARPLUMS

As your eye sweeps toward the adjoining living room fireplace, the family's gold trophies flank the gorgeous mirror that is the centerpiece of the hearth. The dried and painted broomcorn from her grandfather's acreage outside Topeka, Kansas, reflects the love of family and the harvest time that has just passed for this retired farmer. The chocolate Santa on the coffee table is actually a mold for chocolate, not real chocolate that could tempt little children. It is also an acknowledgment of her husband's career with the famous candymaker and an appreciation of all things chocolate this time of year.

Aimee and Mark Sesler's center hall staircase provides a whimsical welcome to all who enter by playfully spelling out Merry Christmas. Aimee purchased these colorful tiles years ago in a seasonal set that includes Happy Halloween, Happy Easter, and Happy Birthday. Her lighted stairwell garland is enhanced by the addition of fresh boxwood greens, clipped to the right lengths, and tucked in around the faux garland that is filled with red berries.

TO THE MANOR

Bring garden architectural elements inside during the winter; it instantly connects us to the outdoors and is uplifting, elevating both our spirits and our accessories.

Nancy Lombardino and Jim McGinness share a wonderful stone, brick, and stucco Tudor that was built in 1923 and is styled in the tradition of the best country manor homes. Nancy loves traditional hunt club fabrics in all shades of red. At the entrance, Nancy used a rich glen plaid ribbon on the wreaths that are mounted on each of her front windows and on her door.

Inside you'll find that their home's rich golden oak woodwork and crown molding, true divided light windows, and architectural fittings are perfectly suitable for their love of equestrian fabrics blended with Western ranching traditions. Not only are you instantly at home in this rich setting, but you're welcomed by the warm tones of their country manor style.

In the entrance to this stately two-story, Nancy—who is the manager of my store in Kansas City—placed an oversized blue willowware vase on a massive garden urn to create the kind of drama that this home demands. The arrangement is filled with evergreens, branches, and feathers. Bold red berries repeat the accent colors of the room, branches, and feathers. With the same ribbon that she used on the outside wreaths, Nancy repeats the pattern inside on the brass wall sconce that is designed in the style of traditional English manors. The garden urn theme is repeated by the fireplace, where Nancy stores her firewood in another very large garden urn. Sitting by the fire, next to the beauty of that gorgeous birch wood, is enough to warm my heart.

CITY CHIC

Melanie and Dave Krumbholz's small twelfth-floor Kansas City apartment that overlooks the Country Club Plaza, an area famous for its holiday lighting ceremony on Thanksgiving, delivers sophisticated style in a small space. When my dear friend Melanie became my assistant at the new Nell Hill's store, she and her husband wanted a shorter commute. They planned this demure space to fit the needs of empty nesters with two grown children. They proved skillful at packing a large amount of style in every square foot. The architectural details, like the curved archways between the living spaces, give the impression that the space is much larger than its blueprint.

Melanie has gathered her hostess gifts on the ottoman in her cozy north-facing sitting room that is equipped with a sectional sofa that fills the space. A large glass cylinder vase holds branches of flowering quince that were found at the local flower market. Forcing spring-blooming branches is very easy—just cut the stems at a diagonal and place in clear water that you change frequently. When you change the water, give the branches another gentle cut on the diagonal. These sweet blooms add to the holiday mood of the dinner party she is hosting for close friends. A tiny Christmas tree next to the sofa is the only other reminder that there is a holiday mood in the air.

Suite!

Around the corner from the sitting room, you'll find the only bedroom in this one-thousand-square-foot layout, but it's a retreat that delivers everything you want in a comfortable master bedroom. For the holidays, it is decked out in simple style with a blue juniper wreath tied to the bedpost of this king-sized bed. Blue juniper berries contrast nicely with Melanie's choice of serene blue wall color. The warm brown hue and ecru of the bedding provide a warm winter tone to the room.

Adjoining this space is one of the classiest bathrooms I've encountered. The marble floor sparkles with tiles that complement the glass knobs on the creamy white cabinets. For the party, the room is lit up with pillar candles on glass pedestals. Boughs of fresh greens are tucked in loosely around the candles.

GOLD AND GLASS

Back at the black-and-white ranch home, my friend Ann keeps it fresh at the entry as she welcomes her ladies' garden club to celebrate the holidays. On the silver candelabra she adds tufts of reindeer moss—one of my favorite elements this season—and swags a fresh green garland with gold-etched glass balls over her gilded mirror. Ann layers a vintage botanical print into the mix with a frame that adds a little touch of black to the scene. A small bouquet highlights a fresh white hydrangea, white salvia (also known as loosestrife), and a few tendrils of seeded eucalyptus.

Fresh and Clean

Right inside the door to her new family room addition, Ann sets the mood with a holiday tray that holds a lone vintage keepsake ornament—a gift from her neighbor—set carefully on a tuft of reindeer moss. The glass urn is sweet with its fresh green apple, kale, flowers, and forced amaryllis bulbs. Tucking in a few naked branches adds just the right amount of height and reminds us that it is still winter.

NATURAL BEAUTY

Ann and Guy found this wonderful antique gold mirror with lights at an estate sale in their hometown of St. Joseph, Missouri. I can't imagine the home it came from, but to me it has always belonged here in Ann's living room. The lights were specially wired behind the mirror. The theme for Ann's garden party is fresh green—from the apples to the paperwhites to the moss. Two little white crocus bulbs are tucked into this scene, along with the silver votives that add a little extra sparkle. I don't think the holidays are complete without some paperwhites somewhere in the plan. Ann started these bulbs two weeks and three weeks before the party so that they would be in various stages of bloom. The amaryllis bulbs take much longer to bloom and become quite large. By putting all the stems and bulbs in glass, Ann adds more greenery to the scene and sets the mood for her holiday table and tree.

BLACK GARDEN URNS
BELONG INSIDE IN
THE WINTER.

PART THREE

The Star of the Show

Gilded Gifts of Nature

We love tradition, but we want to reinvent our customs with our own families.

These beautiful branches retell our Christmas stories and speak of our traditions each year as we prepare for the exchange of gifts—material gifts and the personal gifts of ourselves. For some of us, our traditions around the Christmas tree have been handed down through the generations and date back to our ancestors from other countries and cultures. For some, this might mean selecting the tree on Christmas Eve. For others, the holiday might start on Thanksgiving, as mine does, when my sister Judy arrives for a pre-Christmas visit. I know people who launch the season with a cookie exchange. For others it might be an open house for family and friends.

One thing I do know from talking with friends and customers: We love tradition, but we want to reinvent our customs with our own families. I know one family who gathers for Christmas Eve dinner every year before the grown children scatter to other celebrations. They turn out all the lights and eat by candlelight and the light of the Christmas tree. They always have the same menu, and the children exchange gifts among themselves, something that they have been doing since early childhood. At another household, Santa sneaks into their home during Christmas Eve dinner and leaves all the presents quietly under the tree, much to the delight of the young children who never saw him come in.

As I reimagined my Christmas tree this year, I kept flirting with giant sugar pinecones and decided to cover my tree in these gilded gifts of nature. I located the tree in my customary spot in the living room on a round pedestal table that separates my long living room into two sections. Around the light cord that leads to the tree, I wrapped a loose pine garland and let it drape naturally to the outlet on the wall, as if it is trailing from the tree.

Wrapped in the Warm Glow

Underneath the tree, I imagine the space filled with various sizes and shapes of glass cloches resting on silver trays. Under the glass are placed beautiful ribbons that are picked out for the packages. These ribbons, in all styles and sizes, visually tell the story of a gift list in progress for the visitors who stop by to tour the holiday open house. Even a simple black gift bag makes my heart sing when it is tied with a cream-and-black-striped ribbon cut with pinking scissors. I have stayed with monochromatic wrapping paper through the years, not only because I am somewhat time challenged when it comes to wrapping gifts but also because I just love ribbons. A package can be made special with the addition of an antique spoon, vintage brooch, small picture frame, or special holiday ornament. A friend who gives her adult children money, along with a few other goodies, wraps the cash in many lavish packages and tops the box with a little something personal. She loves to throw them off guard each year, reinventing how to present their gifts.

At night, the shimmer of the tree lights on the glass and silver underneath casts a warm golden glow throughout the room. It reminds me of the Irish tradition of the Garrity ancestry, where it was customary to keep a light burning in every window for travelers to find their way home. For me, the twinkling lights are a welcome sign after busy days at my three shops, and this particular tree provides one of my all-time favorite visual delights. The sight of it is like the relaxing feeling I get after a spa visit—also a once-a-year event!

WINTER WONDERLAND

If my friend Cynthia were to open a bed and breakfast, I know that I would book this room whenever I could get on the waiting list. This masterful blend of whites is as soothing in the winter as it is crisp in the summer. The lightweight Noble fir tucked into the corner and elevated on an antique chair is placed lovingly in wait for the arrival of her daughter for a holiday visit. The simple vintage tree ornaments hung by lightweight gold ribbon complement Cynthia's framed botanical artworks that hang behind the tree in their own gold frames.

SETTLE IN FOR A LONG WINTER'S NAP.

This tree is lovely just for being a beautiful tree. The loose branches are not grown to hold much weight, so the collection of miniature plates—sans lighting—is all this beauty needs. The tree is placed in water and then inserted into one of Cynthia's large willowware urns for stability and nourishment. The container is hidden with reindeer moss. A simple wreath is tied on her iron bed, and a white gift trimmed in gold accents awaits the special guest. Cynthia chose a new white quilt to rest on top of her vintage wool coverlet. Who needs a blanket of snow to put them in a holiday mood? I just want to get cozy in this winter wonderland.

Firmly Rooted in Style

THE MORNING LIGHT REFLECTS BEAUTIFULLY OFF THE GLASS VASE THAT IS

POSITIONED NEXT TO THE BED AT THE LADIES' WRITING DESK. IN KEEPING

WITH THE ROOM'S SIMPLICITY, THE ROOT BALL FROM THIS SMALL NORFOLK

PINE TREE IMMERSED IN WATER PROVIDES TEXTURE, EARTHY INTEREST,

AND A BEAUTIFUL REFLECTION IN THE DRESSING TABLE MIRROR.

SURROUNDED BY SOFTNESS

The headboard of the white iron bed is slip-covered in a beautiful white-on-cream monogram, adding the needed softness to the scene. I love decor that mixes metals and rustic materials with refined objects, and this room has exactly the right mix. The reproduction butterfly plates and platter above the bed, also trimmed in gold, instantly tie them to the other gold accents in the room. Adding a spray of fresh evergreens to this scene takes it from its summer roots and clearly identifies it as a holiday retreat. To me, this is a perfect bedroom—it is as homey in summer as it is in winter—and only simple fresh greens change the mood.

THE MANNER OF GIVING

Cynthia's little cottage is a study in contrasts. This inviting guestroom is just down the hall from her all-white retreat, and the deep navy tones set the mood for this very special antique hand-carved bed. Just as her other tree was covered in ornaments only, this fresh bedside Dwarf Blue Spruce tree is only lit with tiny lights. A large ice bucket of bold holiday red metal holds a little balsam tree topper that awaits her son's arrival. Tree toppers—the top part of larger trees that has been removed to fit the tree under the ceilings of our eight- and nine-foot rooms—are a great source for tabletop trees. They are especially prized for their perfect symmetry. The monogram on the pillow sham reflects her husband's initials, and the desk in this well-designed room has become a wrapping station in the days before her guests arrive.

Cynthia is masterful at framing art. She loves to travel, and on one trip she fell in love with this historical print collection, just because. She knew exactly how these would look in the right room and in the right frames. She found these years before they worked their way into this cottage retreat. She designs her own mattes and frames with the help of a local crafts store that carries an excellent selection of affordable ready-made frames.

After she has wrapped her small welcome gifts, she tucks them on the sconce across from the bed, where they will be discovered by her guest—her son. Hiding welcome gifts for company is a festive way to begin a visit.

AND THE TROPHY GOES TO . . .

The warm rich plaids, paisleys, and pomegranate shades that make up Nancy and Jim's very special living room reflect their colorful heritage and love of horses, dogs, and the first-class trapshooting skills of Jim's father. When I first visited their home, my eye was drawn to this very special trophy with its horn handles, presented in 1956 to Jim's father, Bob McGinness, for the Missouri-Kansas state championship in trapshooting.

I knew it had to be the centerpiece for their holiday floral arrangement. Elevating it to a position of importance in the room, next to some of their favorite books, tells a story about the past generation and keeps memories of this story close to family members' hearts. Christmas is the perfect time to honor the past, making it timeless for all generations. This very special trophy is a tribute to their heritage and all they hold dear.

TELL ME A STORY

When I walked into Aimee's living room I immediately appreciated the masterful way she assembled the various layers and textures of her tree. She definitely has a keen sense for how a tree should be presented to the world. As is her tradition, she adorned the tree with her favorite golden and glass ornaments, of various shapes and sizes but uniform in their color tones. This year, however, she told a new story. While picking broomcorn with her young children on her grandfather's acreage this past autumn, she was inspired to bring bunches of this native sorghum home for her tree, to bring something special from his farming roots into her holiday storytelling. She dried the stalks, spray-painted them a light metallic so that they would hold their form, tied them off with twine, and lay them in bunches between the branches of her tree, on her mantel, and in her holiday arrangements. It

was the perfect way to re-create her tradition of capturing a natural look by wrapping grapevine branches around the outside of her tree after all the ornaments are in place. The broomcorn gives the tree depth and reminds her daily of this important person in her life.

Six Simple Steps to Layering a Tree

My friend Kelly loves fresh trees and says that her tree trimming is more like tree stuffing. In her workshop on decorating Christmas trees, she breaks the process down by starting out with these rules:

- Plan on one hundred lights for each foot of the tree's height (an eight-foot tree should have at least eight hundred lights).

- Don't shove the tree in the first available corner. Create a space for your masterpiece. After all, it is the *prima donna* of your plan.

- Use a tablecloth in place of a tree skirt. It will probably be less expensive, and most of them are made to be easily laundered afterward. They also are made of fabrics that drape easily.

- Above all else, pick a theme and stick with it. Whether it's woodsy with grapevine garland, birds' nests, and touches of fresh or dried hydrangea or an eclectic collection of handmade ornaments, pick a color palette and overarching theme to hold it all together.

- Absolutely *do not* have more than three colors in your palette. More than this becomes uncontrollable and chaotic.

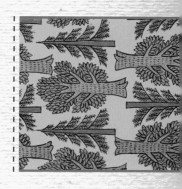

THE SIX-LAYER TREE

Think of your tree as a six-layer cake. If you pay attention to this concept, you will not fail, and your tree will become a conversation piece. Here are the layers and details on how to decorate each layer.

LAYER 1.
THE TOP: LIGHTS AND GARLAND
FIRST, FROM THE TOP DOWN

Spend time on this base decor because this is the most important step in getting your look. Make sure that your lights are evenly distributed from top to bottom. Add the best element of your theme on layer 1, such as grapevine beginning at the top and winding its way through the branches to the bottom. Or maybe it's a wide ribbon that you purchased just for the tree. It could be garlands of berries, fresh cranberries, or popcorn strings, but get this layer in place first.

LAYER 2.
THE MIDDLE OF THE TREE:
PLACE BIG THEME ITEMS

Start at the middle of the tree and add big-ticket items such as giant pinecones, china dolls, stuffed Santas, or giant stars or snowflakes. After you have decided on the balance at the center of the tree, add one of these large objects to the top and two or three around the base.

LAYER 3.
THE BOTTOM OF THE TREE:
TAKE IT TO NEW HEIGHTS

I personally enjoy adding another element to my theme by gathering sticks or stems of silk flowers, dried hydrangeas, or something textural that fits the overall garland. This layer is optional, depending on your theme.

LAYER 4.
INSIDE THE TREE BRANCHES:
CREATE A CONVERSATION PIECE

Framed family photos add personality, tucked in or hung with ribbons that match your color palette. Gingerbread cookies that have been baked and glazed add earth tones, or more colorful white sugar cookies with bursts of colorful centers can provide homemade sizzle (make sure they don't get ingested by unknowing visitors: rodent, canine, cats, or human). Add monograms to your cookie creations to further personalize your tree. Or hang monogrammed ornaments that are purchased, one for each family member.

LAYER 5.
EDGE OF THE BRANCHES:
CREATE DEPTH AND DIMENSION

Tuck in birds' nests, dried artichokes, or silk pears, or use your basic color-based ornaments here to give the tree a depth of color that is subtle but creates an overall impression. This is the layer where you want to tuck in the ornaments that are meaningful and necessary but not exactly your favorites (hide them a bit).

LAYER 6.
OUTSIDE OF THE TREE:
THE FUN FINISH

Here's where to go nuts, if your tree is over the top. Throw your tinsel into the air and drape the entire tree, letting it catch where it falls. Or tie little golden or silver bows to the very tips of the branches to give your tree extra sparkle.

CITY CHRISTMAS

Melanie and Dave's balcony overlooking the Plaza shopping district provides a dreamy setting in which to share a holiday dinner with friends. This black garden urn serves as a container garden year-round, but on this magical evening it holds a fresh Alberta Spruce Christmas tree filled with lights and fresh hydrangea blooms. The garland criss-crossing behind the tree is made of Belles of Ireland, strung together and attached to the glass balcony wall. The twinkling tree lights combine with the twinkle of the city lights to offer guests an intimate holiday dinner setting.

GREEN WITH ENVY

I love black and white in my decorating plan, but when it comes to black and white at Ann Humphrey's house, I find myself green with envy. She is masterful in the way she seemingly effortlessly mixes this color scheme into everything she does. But it never looks repetitious, and it is always imaginative. For this holiday party she hosted for her garden club, she chose apple green as her main accent color. I never imagined that black Christmas presents could make everything around them stand out with such command of the holiday. I love these giant balls tucked into her loose and whimsical tree. The smoky black screen behind the tree ensures that it will be noticed. It gives the cream-colored iron base and white club chair next to the tree the needed contrast for this special corner.

Take a Bow

The holidays are all the more special because we exchange gifts with loved ones, dear friends, and neighbors. But the manner of giving is also important and the way we wrap our presents communicates that others are special. I have learned so much from friends and customers over the years about keeping the basics of wrapping simple.

For example, I still stand by my rule of using kraft paper as much as possible. It is the color of nature, which is a source of endless inspiration for my decor. Every color ribbon imaginable looks good with kraft paper. In fact, coordinating your ribbon with your holiday color scheme is just as important as the tree. Another easy, but stylish approach is to use premade boxes. My friend Nancy punched two holes in the lid of this larger box and looped a beautiful ribbon through the holes. She then packed it with homemade cookies, adding beautiful ribbons to the boxes for the "wow" factor. On top of your packages, tuck in feathers or gilded leaves. Use a glue gun to attach pinecones or little birds' nests. A brooch pinned to the ribbon or a small bracelet intertwined with the ribbon is a beautiful way to surprise a girlfriend. A charm for a necklace or a pair of dangly earrings is also a stylish way to dress up a gift.

Hostess gifts are wonderful ways to use fresh ingredients, like moss or fresh floral stems from the centerpiece. Look around your home for inspiration. It is also fun to look for packaging that becomes part of the gift, like natural woven baskets with lids that can contain homemade goodies, or a new set of garden tools for the gardener in your life. Little craft boxes from the hobby store are also excellent containers to embellish.

DRESS THE SMALLEST GIFT IN HOLIDAY FANCY.

DREAMS OF DESSERT DANCE IN MY HEAD

I AM DREAMING OF DESSERT WITH DAVID AFTER I

EXPERIENCED THE ULTIMATE DESSERT DRAMA—IT

WAS MORE LIKE A DESSERT PROM—AT THE HOME OF

DAVID JIMENEZ. HE CREATED THIS SOPHISTICATED

PARTY PLAN FOR HOSTING LATE-NIGHT SWEETS

ON THE SIDE PORTICO OF HIS HISTORIC HOME

IN THE HYDE PARK NEIGHBORHOOD OF KANSAS

CITY, WHERE HE LOVES TO ENTERTAIN LARGE

GATHERINGS. FOR THIS FANCIFUL DESSERT PARTY,

DAVID BEGAN BY WRAPPING THE VERTICALLY

CARVED COLONNADES ON THIS CLASSICALLY BUILT

PORCH WITH HORIZONTAL GARLANDS. THESE ARE

BEAUTIFUL PILLARS IN THEIR OWN RIGHT, BUT

THEY TAKE ON MAGICAL PROPORTIONS WHEN

DECORATED AND LIGHTED FOR CHRISTMAS.

A CANDY STORE CHRISTMAS

I walked through my store with David as he was planning this event, and I sent him some of my favorite accent pieces to work with, including the large black urn that holds the most beautiful fresh floral tree with its white lilies, giant white hydrangea, red berries, and assortment of fresh evergreens. In fact, as I studied this fresh arrangement, I spotted all my favorite evergreen varieties. David then worked with his favorite baker to create these dreamy white and cream-colored meringue cakes and cookies, which add an ethereal element that looks as if angels dropped dollops of fresh meringue from the sky. He put layered cakes and cookies under small glass cloches on risers and then tied black-and-cream-striped ribbons around the stems of a few of the risers to give them special treatment on the dessert table.

I like to create a visual treat for my guests.

—DAVID JIMENEZ

I love that David's porch is an extension of his interior design, with leather wing chairs, black-and-white-striped fabrics, and a mix of tabletop materials and designs, including glass, metal, and marble. On the wall of his porch, against the light brick background, a large black iron screen is anchored to define the seating space and unify the black-and-white theme of the floor tiles, furniture, and outdoor fabrics. The lanterns encircling the scene enhance the glow of the holidays in the air. David's visual art experience is legendary, having been the visual director of the design of Pottery Barn and Restoration Hardware. He brought his talents to Hallmark Cards, and I have been lucky enough to have him design an entertaining event that put me in what I'm now calling "The David Zone."

CHAMPAGNE, ANYONE?

When David traveled to his native New York to visit family at Thanksgiving, he stopped at his favorite confectioner's, Dylan's Candy Bar, where he picked out their famous ribbon candy in both curls and wheels, adding peppermint sticks and red hots for just the right accents. Using glass apothecary jars from my store, he set about building his own candy store on the side porch. He added white chocolate–covered pretzels and vanilla Jelly Bellies, in keeping with his color scheme of all shades of harmonious whites and creams. Vases of bright red roses accented with berries contrast with the pale shades to give the right amount of Christmas color to this wintry white scene.

The pièce de résistance is his friend Merrily's dreamy white coconut layer cake, which they frosted together over drinks the night before the party, using fresh coconut shavings to create this large, perfect snowball dessert.

TAKE THE PARTY

OUTSIDE.

PART FOUR

The Celebration

A Sensory Feast

No holiday engages our senses more than Christmas. The stores and streets are filled with sounds of music and bell-ringing, and we are surrounded by visual treats everywhere we look. Even with all this bustling activity everywhere we go, nothing compares to the aromas we associate with this season. From the turkey and stuffing that kick off the celebration to firewood, cinnamon, nutmeg, and pine, subtle scents fill the air and surround us with instant memories of holidays past. Smell evokes powerful memories, and it's all a wonderful part of this time of year.

One thing that makes my heart beat faster is seeing all the dishes, cutlery, glassware, and accoutrements that go into preparing a fabulous meal, a fantastic table, and a warm and easy place for friends and family to kick off a memorable evening over cocktails that will linger well into the evening over coffee and dessert. When I undertook the remodeling of the kitchen in our 130-year-old home, I was working with very limited floor space, especially in the cook's area (that would be for my husband). Last year, I added this service island that could hold my favorite large chargers. In the fall, I put my silver turkey platter and dome out in preparation for the big days of feasting that are just around the corner. Fresh pomegranates lining the windowsill—so delicious in decorating—made their way into a new drink that my daughter mixed for us on Christmas. The newest member of the household, Kitty Couscous, likes to play hide-and-seek among the chargers.

DRESSING THE CUPBOARD

The breakfast area, which makes up the larger part of my kitchen space, holds two French chairs, a gift to myself this year. They are upholstered in mixed fabrics: a toile backing on the front, with vintage brown florals on the back and seats in coordinating mattress ticking. All of the fabrics are separated yet coordinated with braided piping attached to the outside rims. Fresh pink tulips and lipstick pink mugs match the stripes in the candy canes and the delicate pink trim around the vintage tablecloth. I love areas that do double-duty. This is where we watch morning and evening news and catch a late-night supper. But for me, the beauty of it all is that I can see many of my favorite things in the glass-front cabinets—something that makes my heart sing.

If Christmas trees are the keepers of our family's memories, then certainly the feasts, parties, luncheons, buffets, and open houses that go along with the holiday season are an integral part of telling our stories. Throughout our lives, in prosperous times and otherwise, the giving and sharing of food is the most symbolic gesture of love and care that we show each other. Everyday food shifts into holiday mode as you plan how you want to set your tables, entertain your family and friends, and bake for neighbors and coworkers. A simple bowl of nuts can instantly and subtly say it's a holiday, and a more elaborate fruit arrangement tells visitors that this kitchen is ready for a special time of year.

FIRESIDE CHATS

One of my philosophies of entertaining is to keep all the prized possessions that you love—either new-found or handed down from previous generations—close at hand and available for use year-round. Why not use something beautiful and meaningful in your holiday plans? No person is more meaningful to me at the holidays than my big sister, Judy. Judy is an editor at the *Detroit News* and her deadlines rarely allow for long absences from her work. Her annual visit is the highlight of my festivities, and when she is close at hand, I am ready for the transition from shopkeeper to little sister. This year I imagined Judy's visit and set about in the liv-

ing room to create an intimate and cozy dinner setting for two.

My faithful gold dishes and pearl-handled knives set the mood at a table for two in front of my fireplace. The centerpiece is a silver epergne that was love at first sight. The lower level of this beauty holds fresh fruit—something that we must use in our decorating this time of year. The top flute holds a bouquet of white roses, hydrangea heads, and loosestrife, and white roses are repeated in petite arrangements in front of each place setting. Fresh greens are tucked in for texture and give the scene a relaxed elegance.

ORGANIC DECORATING

In the history of Christmas traditions, the gift of fruit holds an important position in our customs. Receiving fruit in our stockings dates back to earlier times when it was hard to find fruit in the winter, and one orange was truly a rare treat. High prices were paid for fresh foods that had to come long distances to arrive at our Christmas doors. The use of fruit today is still an honored tradition that you'll find at Christmas celebrations and a symbol of the bountiful gifts of the season.

To me, fresh produce can be just as beautiful to look at as newly picked flowers from the garden. Fruit adds texture and color to the table, too, and is easy to arrange because it looks so pretty just stacked up, and it is reusable after the party is over.

So many holiday shoppers at Nell Hill's are looking for quick stocking stuffers, teachers' gifts, treats for gift exchanges, or affordable gifts for their bridge or bunko clubs. In setting up this ladies' holiday luncheon at the town home, in keeping with the theme of fresh produce, we encircled the necks of the concrete busts with a wreath made from magnolia leaves—the same magnolia that we carried throughout the great room that adjoins the kitchen. A large woven wicker tray serves as a charger for this place setting, and the place cards are attached to the linen napkins with small gold frames. The garden busts and frames will go home with the ladies as gifts from the hostess.

Everyone at this gathering will also receive a small fresh

rosemary pot wrapped in burlap, along with a gift box that

contains chocolates. These small, ready-made craft boxes are

an easy, affordable way to dress up your gifts.

What a Dish!

I have fallen in love with so many dishes at first sight. Many of them are now in my cupboards, but others I have coveted in the homes of my friends. There is no better time to show off your dishware than at the holidays, although, I must tell you, I am big on using my best dishes year round. What good are they if they stay inside your cabinets 360 days out of the year?

These three black-and-white pattern dishes are from my dishware line and the patterns were inspired by eighteenth-century French fabric swatches. We reproduced the designs in contemporary materials. The dinner plate is layered with a large cream salad plate in a relief pattern, followed by an appetizer plate and floral dessert plate on top. The large silver tray serves as a charger. The black-and-white napkin with crewel is festive and perfect for the black-and-white party on page 107.

For more casual holiday luncheons, consider using a wicker tray, topped with a black-and-white transfer ware dinner plate. The one pictured here is layered with a soup tureen and the coordinating napkin is looped through the handle of the tray—a style we favor at Nell Hill's. Each place setting holds a Christmas card from the hostess with an uplifting holiday message.

Everyone needs a basic set of white dishes and these simple ones with black rims and a bird relief pattern are the workhorses of my stable. I tell everyone to start with basic white

dishes and this is especially true at the holidays. With white dishes as a backdrop, you can set a snow-white scene that is all about winter. Adding pops of holiday reds and greens, running a plaid runner down the center of the table, or topping each plate with a colorfully wrapped hostess gift—anything is possible with basic white.

The blue-and-white pattern from the home featured on page 104 is called Fruit Basket and is an ironstone plate that was made in England for Mason's. This simple presentation allows the dishes to stand out against the wood of the dining table, and showcases the perfect dishes for a holiday breakfast or brunch.

When I spotted these gold-rimmed lovelies at Nancy Lombardino's house, I knew they were the right ones to use for Nancy's buffet suppers. She collects all shapes and sizes of trays and sets them out in stacks when she has a buffet dinner. I think these little jewels shine their brightest at the holidays, when the lights of the season illuminate their gold-leaf edges and details—they make my heart sing whenever they perform their tableside magic.

These sophisticated plates that feature ships is the pattern "Trade Winds" from Spode and are simply beautiful because they are simple. I could not imagine them anywhere else but in the tailored dining room featured on page 116. Against the molasses walls of the room, their reddish brown color is distinctive and sophisticated. They present a quiet reminder of just how artistic a plate can be—setting an imaginative atmosphere for an entire table.

A Simple Arrangement Sets the Holiday Mood

The use of magnolia as the main accent is repeated in the adjoining kitchen, where a white ironstone pitcher holds large stems punctuated with holly berry. The marble countertop holds a lovely cheese tray conveniently placed between the kitchen and dining room buffet table. Layer the background of the white tiles with a silver tray and artwork to hold the scene together.

A whimsical cow head towers above the room, guarding the cheese. This unexpected ceiling-high accent is here year-round, but decorating it at the holidays with large pinecones and fresh green accents is a nod to the frivolity of the holidays and adds to the casual mood of this buffet supper in progress.

SETTING A BEAUTIFUL BUFFET

Ready-made star-shaped boxes also add style to this dining room buffet. Setting an elegant but simple dining buffet doesn't have to be difficult. Each hostess gift box is decorated with fresh sprigs from the floral arrangements. These simple gifts when decorated become part of the table arrangement.

Fresh sugar stars from a gourmet baking department are sprinkled around the base of the silver serving tray. This little bit of whimsy adds a sparkle to the holiday table. Close by, on the dessert tray, star-shaped sugar cubes wait with the coffee service to sweeten this simple scene.

Fresh sprigs of rosemary are tucked into the silver rim of each faux-alligator napkin ring. For a buffet, this is a clever way for guests to add both color and flavor to their plates when the napkins are unrolled. Choose an herb that goes with the meal; in this case rosemary was chosen to go with sliced beef tenderloin. For an Italian feast, tuck in basil leaves; use cilantro for a Mexican supper.

TIDINGS OF COMFORT AND JOY

The silver lanterns in Aimee Sesler's dining room light the way to a sweet holiday surprise just around the corner in the kitchen. The lanterns are filled with fresh cranberries floating around the base of white pillar candles. I love discovering what Aimee does in her older home because she always does it right, even if that means waiting or going the extra mile on restoration. This gorgeous door between the dining room and kitchen was discovered in the back of her century-old garage. It had to be cut down to fit the new walls and woodwork. The green leaded glass window on this special find complements the green walls in the room, and a large balsam wreath is all this beauty needs to show off.

The same red and white ribbon on her outside gates is repeated here in this simple tableau. Aimee's three children participate in the festivities by frosting—and sampling—the cupcakes that will be offered at one such family get-together. Her kitchen island has been outfitted with all the trimmings for a sweet gathering. Frosted Christmas cookies are placed on risers under Grant's (age 5) watchful eye. The girls Erika (6) and Sophia (2½) help Mom prepare the gift baskets that will be delivered to neighbors in the coming days. The stained concrete counters in Aimee's kitchen are punctuated with deep pink tulips. Reindeer moss wreaths are staggered in two sizes from the glass-front cabinets. Large glass jars on the island hold the many holiday treats that add to the merriment and energy level of this busy household.

Ann's garden luncheon begins at the bar, which is set up in her large kitchen addition off the dining room. Granny Smith apples and large bunches of fresh floral kale are gathered in this silver urn and reflected in the mirror that anchors this area. A mirror is nestled inside the silver serving tray, reflecting the shimmer of the cut glass barware that is ready for her guests. A compote of sugared pecans is offered to sweeten the deal. Notice the lovely lace-patterned bottled water that Ann discovered at a large retail store in her neighborhood.

A Garden in Winter

In keeping with her garden theme, Ann offers a natural tableau on her breakfront next to the buffet table. This cloche spotlights the paperwhite bulbs that are forcing their way to the surface—a reminder to this garden club of their passion for the green things growing. Reindeer moss tufts encircle the arrangement.

On the dining table close by, the flower arrangement gets more dramatic as floating Granny Smith apples meander down the glass cylinder vase that is filled with an abundance of white stems and holiday greenery. The black-and-white plates are ready on the checked table cover that anchors the color palette.

AND THEN IN A TWINKLING

AS NIGHT FALLS ON THIS GATHERING THAT HAS

GONE LATE INTO THE AFTERNOON, ANN'S OUTSIDE

LANTERNS AND LIGHTS FILL THE ROOM WITH THE

MAGICAL MOOD OF THE SEASON, REMINDING THEM

THAT IT IS STILL THE BEGINNING OF WINTER.

FEAST FOR THE EYES

Cynthia is getting ready in her kitchen in the cozy cottage in Atchison. For years, Cynthia has collected English Spode china and blue Staffordshire plates. When she remodeled her kitchen, she tore out the upper cabinets and installed this plate rack that runs from the top of the cabinet bases all the way to the ceiling. She always wanted a place to display her collection of china and old cobalt blue, and it was in this small country kitchen that her dream came to life. Cynthia loves to keep her serving utensils close at hand where she can see them. She prepares for arriving guests by loading a glass compote with fresh grapes, apples, and pears. Salt shakers and pearl-handled knives, glass-handled picks, tiny appetizer forks, silver tongs, and small demitasse spoons are lovingly collected by this classy cook. Fresh sprigs of evergreen in glass bud vases and blue vases whisper, "It's the holidays."

CANINE CHRISTMAS

Cynthia's tiny mudroom off the kitchen is anything but dirty. The only thing here that is muddy is the wall color. This stylish bar is guarded over by the canine patrol, including these classic Staffordshire reproductions that found a permanent home on matching pedestals. The ivy topiary Christmas tree tells visitors that it's Christmas. I love rooms that do double-duty, but this little space is one of the hardest-working rooms I know. The bar top is made from varnished hardwood and holds a curtain over the front that is gathered on brass rings. It hides a front-loading washer and dryer underneath.

Best of Show

The black-and-white tile makes cleanup easy because this is where Cynthia serves her two canines on a special willowware platter. The dog pastries were purchased from a dog bakery for a lot less money than you might imagine—just a few dollars. The glass-front antique kitchen cabinet stores essentials for entertaining in this cottage retreat, and the iron Scottie, with a tiny silver bell holiday collar, stands at attention for this best-of-show inspection.

AND THE FIRST PLACE RIBBON GOES TO . . .

If Cynthia has gone to the dogs, then you can count on Nancy and Jim being most at home on the range. The cattle-ranching skills of Jim's father are honored and celebrated in their home. Jim's father's ranch, the MM Ranch in Lathrop, Missouri, pioneered the Charolais breed of cattle in North America during the late 1940s. The martini bar includes another commemorative trophy, a Grand American Championship Shoot awarded in 1956, that is repurposed here as an ice bucket. I believe in using your most valuable pieces, especially at the holidays, whether they are prized for their value or their sentimentality. The tray underneath holds cocktail onions that are soaked in vermouth and tiny, tart cornichon pickles, great accompaniments for mixing martinis.

In a nearby breakfast room, the silver deer–handled punch bowl was a gift from Nancy's sister. Its large size favors the making of a citrus-flavored concoction. Rustic spurs are added to the greenery that fills the top of the serving tray. Jim bought the commemorative collection cowboy plates that were produced by Wallace China in the 1950s just because he loved them.

When I entertain for the holidays—for any event, really—my secret is to prepare ahead of time. The hostess gifts are wrapped and ready on a tray that sits atop a linen-covered slipper chair. Staying with simple two-color themes on packages ensures that they will blend with the decor of the party. On these packages, Nancy chose paper in the color of her dining room walls. You might not think of brown as a holiday color—that is, not until you add fresh moss green satin ribbon, gold accents, and sprigs of fresh winter greens.

RUSTIC ROMANCE

A relaxing treat bar contains multiple flavors and choices for sampling by guests. The framed white suede chaps from Jim's father are allowed to own this room, in tribute to his extraordinary livestock and ranching skills. To dramatize this nod to his heritage, massive antler candelabra anchor either end of the buffet. Large taper candles add even more vertical drama. The rustic garden urn is filled with feathers, and draped over the edge are a pair of nail-studded chaps that were a gift to Jim when he was a young cowboy on his father's working ranch.

Imported cheeses, freshly baked bread, sugared pineapple rings, sweet dried ginger for refreshment, large blocks of dark chocolate awaiting discovery, miniature bananas, and fresh fruits of many varieties decorate the casual sideboard that has been garnished with some of the season's best offerings.

THE LOOK OF LEATHER

The drama is heightened at the dining table, where a plaid tablecloth holds delicate plates on faux-leather chargers and shiny trays. The red roses and tulips in the centerpieces and candelabra with antler are elevated enough so that the host and hostess can see everyone from their vantage point on the monogrammed bench that is centered at the head of the table. It's a long way from the chuckwagon but still is a casually elegant way to celebrate the cowboy culture and in keeping with the family traditions of this household.

FOR NANCY AND JIM'S GATHERING, A CABINET IN THE DINING ROOM IS
SET UP FOR AFTER-DINNER DRINKS WITH BEAUTIFUL PARROT TULIPS AND
SPRAY ROSES IN TROPHY CUPS. SMALL CORDIAL GLASSES ON A SILVER TRAY
AND PEPPERMINT STICKS AND CHOCOLATE-COVERED SWIZZLE STICKS
DECORATE THE SAUCERS OF THE COFFEE CUPS STACKED AND READY FOR
COMPANY. THE LARGER SUGAR SHAKER, ALONGSIDE FRESH CINNAMON
STICKS, HOLDS GROUND CINNAMON FOR A HOLIDAY SPLASH.

A GLAMOROUS HOLIDAY

Customers and friends often tell me that they are baffled at the
holidays when it comes to smaller living spaces. Not all of us can fit
a large tree in our spaces, so thinking about every space you have becomes paramount in your decisions on how to decorate. For example,
Melanie hung a very hearty, fanciful wreath on her mirror over her
bar service. The wreath is one of my favorites in terms of mixing different elements in a soft, sophisticated way. Just by adding two floral
ribbons—one gold in a four-inch width and one in deep pomegranate in a two-inch width—Melanie achieved a large holiday statement
without using up any of her square footage. She also fits a very stylish
bar service in a small space between her balcony and hallway.

Just around the corner, this wonderful angel watches over guests in the guest bath, where this holiday arrangement sets a festive tone. This garden statue looks as if she is wearing a cape made of pine needles. I lust after Melanie's gold mirror with tendrils winding their way up to the bird sitting on top.

Melanie's table is drenched in subtle sophistication. Her glass chandelier is the showstopper in this arrangement, where she suspended three large, etched glass ornaments on pomegranate-colored floral ribbons. The floral centerpiece is made up of tea roses and hydrangea, but to make it look holiday-ready, there are stems of fresh evergreen tucked in with the lighter florals. The arrangement is placed in a large antique silver urn and elevated slightly on a square silver pedestal. Each plate has a lovely glass compote filled with not soup or salad, but a miniature collection of flowers that becomes the individual decoration at each place setting. Bone-handled appetizer knives and forks are crisscrossed on top of each place setting, awaiting the first course selection.

The kitchen island is a masterful hand-carved wooden counter that adds furniture style to the great room area. The large, slender gold-detailed candelabra are filled with votive cups of fresh flowers and greens that tower above the surface. This brings the eye up in the room, and the greens in the arrangements provide the holiday atmosphere that is needed this time of year. This is yet another alternative to using fresh swags on the chandelier over the island. Melanie can make use of these candelabra throughout the year—whether she is dining by candlelight or dressing them up, as she has done here, for a special holiday celebration. It is important to establish your style at Christmas by using the accessories you love year-round, but giving these objects importance in your holiday settings.

Another example of elevating beloved keepsakes is illustrated in the antique silver coffee urn that Melanie spotted at an estate sale and her friends talked her into buying. The little floral arrangement on the counter is actually gathered inside a small sugar service. Notice the tiny sugar scoop that sits alongside the flowers on the marble counter.

Goodies

Every holiday gathering showcases food in some way or another. It can be as simple as a bowl of beautiful nuts or fresh fruit, or as decadent as the finest chocolates with brandy or champagne. At the end of Melanie's special evening, she served this mocha chocolate cake, decorated with chocolate swirls and fresh eucalyptus leaves tucked in the sides. Bright orange clementines with chocolate-covered apricots play with the colors of the tulips to create a mood that is comfortable and natural like the cinnamon sticks and pistachios—just how we want our guests to feel when we entertain.

HOW SWEET
IT IS!

The Colorful Moods of Christmas

*May you have the
gladness of Christmas
which is hope;
The spirit of Christmas
which is peace;
The heart of Christmas
which is love.*

—ADA V. HENDRICKS

Resources

Most of the accessories featured in this book, unless otherwise noted, are from Mary Carol Garrity's stores. For complete information on her stores that specialize in home furnishings and accents, visit www.nellhills.com. For additional information on the Mary Carol Home Collection, a complete line of home decor products, contact the Gerson Company at www.gersoncompany.com.

NELL HILL'S/ATCHISON
501 Commercial Street
Atchison, KS 66002
(913) 367-1086
Gifts, accessories, furniture, and tabletop

NELL HILL'S/KANSAS CITY
Briarcliff Village
4101 North Mulberry Drive
Kansas City, MO 64116
Fabric, bedding, gifts, accessories, furniture, and tabletop

GARRITY'S ENCORE
121 North Fifth Street
Atchison, KS 66002
Gifts, accessories, furniture, tabletop, and sale items

This book would not have been possible without the help and services of many professionals in their respective fields of expertise. Every effort has been made to recognize them here.

FLORISTS

Charles Matney
(Home of David Jimenez)
Matney Floral Designs
2708 West Fifty-third Street
Fairway, KS 66205
(913) 362-5419

Shana Vaughn
(Krumbholz' home and Lombardino/McGinness home)
Shana Vaughn Designs
(816) 914-4257
www.shanavaughndesigns.com

Kelly Acock
(All other homes featured)
Anne Kelly Company
www.annekellycompany.com

RETAIL STORES

Dean & DeLuca
4700 West 119th Street
Leawood, KS 66209
(913) 498-3131

The Better Cheddar
Prairie Village Shopping Center
#5 On the Mall (Seventy-first and Mission Road)
Prairie Village, KS 66208
(913) 362-7575

Three Dog Bakery
Country Club Plaza
612 West Forty-eighth Street
Kansas City, MO 64112
(816) 753-3647

The Paper Source
Country Club Plaza
621 West Forty-eighth Street
Kansas City, MO 64112
(816) 753-2777

CANDY AND CONFECTIONERS

Dylan's Candy Bar
1011 Third Avenue
New York, NY 10021
(646) 735-0078

Natasha Goellner
(Home of David Jimenez)
Natasha's Mulberry and Mott
French Pastries and Desserts
10573 Mission Road
Leawood, KS 66206

Andres Confiserie Suisse
5018 Main Street
Kansas City, MO 64112
(816) 561-6484
(800) 892-1234

SEAMSTRESS

Stockings by Diane Sudhoff
South House Design
1239 Parkdale
Maryville, MO 64468
(660) 582-8182

Kelly Wilson
Weave Gotcha Covered!
weavegotchacovered@kc.rr.com

Acknowledgments

A special thanks, from the bottom of my heart, goes out to those home-owners who generously shared their creative talents to make this book possible. It's not easy to have your home taken over by a photo crew, especially during the holidays. I especially want to acknowledge their special contributions. Thanks to Maggie Fisher and Katie Gerson of Revival Development, the owners and designers of the reproduction town home. Ann and Guy Humphreys and their fan club in St. Joseph, Missouri, provided their customary hospitality and generous spirits when they invited us to their ranch home—and even provided the beginnings of a winter storm to go with it. Cynthia and Tom Hoenig's Atchison cottage is always one of my favorite creative hideaways—and never more than at Christmas-time. I am grateful to David Jimenez for sharing his immense talents at his historic midwestern colonial home and his wonderful friend and entertainment writer Merrily Jackson. Aimee and Mark Sesler not only shared their English Tudor home with us, but charmed us with their three children, Erika, Grant, and Sophia. A special thanks to my store manager Nancy

Lombardino and Jim McGinness for opening up their traditional manor home and sharing their wonderful stories. And finally, to Melanie and David Krumbholz and their amazing Plaza apartment. Melanie's stylish home goes with her overall style and grace. I want to thank those people who worked extra hard to make this book possible, especially editorial director Jean Lowe and photographer Bob Greenspan, who put their collaborative creative talents to this project, and for the creative styling of Cheryl Owens, Cecelia Pellettiere, Kelly Acock, Shana Vaughn, and Dillon Kinsman. Special thanks to Melody McKeever at C.R. Laine. Thanks to the Gerson Companies for their contributions: Liz Hjalmarson, Lonte Wires, Nancy Denny, Sandy Paylor-Westra, and Amanda Reynolds

Thank you to the publishing team at Andrews McMeel Publishing for their support: Hugh Andrews and Kirsty Melville, editor Dorothy O'Brien and her talented designers Julie Barnes and Diane Marsh, and Kathy Hilliard for promoting the book.

None of this would be possible without my dedicated, faithful store employees and friends whose contributions to making Nell Hill's

successful are immeasurable. I am so grateful to them for their help and talent. They are as follows: Melinda Allaman, Kim Amick, Kathleen Armstrong, Glenna Botchelder, Marsee Bates, George Bilimek, LuAnn Bownik, Carolyn Campbell, Ethel Campbell, Joan Carpenter, Gloria Case, Shirley Cline, Joyce Coleman, Lynda Coulter, Jerry Cross, Carey DeBasio, Jason DeJonge, Melinda DiCarlo, Joe Domann, Deann Dunn, Dee Dee Dunn, Pamela Dunn, Robin Enright, Anne Epstein, Barb Fricke, Pamela Gibson, Deanna Gilbert, Brenda Graves, Judy Green, Amy Harris, Lori Harris, Angela Harris-Spurlock, Sherry Hartshorn, Marla Heavin, Vicki Hinde, Kim Hobbs, Cynthia Hoenig, Lauren Holderby, Diane Howard, Ann Humphreys, John Hysten, Nancy Jones, Cathy Kirkpatrick, Cali Kliewer, Pat Kuckelman, Andrea Kuhnert,

Beth Langer, Jane Law, Mark Leonardi, Delores Limpic, Mary Lu Liolios, Richard Lippincott, Janet Lohnes, Nancy Lombardino, June Lynn, Michelle McCarthy, Meghan McCreary, Kathy McLean, Brett Miner, Stacey Miner, Amy Minnis, Shannon Mize, Gloria Nash, Nancy Neary, Patti Newsom, Lois Niemann, Kenneth Otte, Donna Pierson, Christine Renner, Geraldine Rhodes, Fanny Sansone, Vickie Scholz, Alice Scott, Crystal See, Beau Shamet, Dorothy Speer, Gretchen Sullivan, Lilli Taylor, Rebecca Taylor, Diane Tomlinson, Virginia Voelker, Ginny Voss, Terry Voss, Tina Welch, Macy White, Lindsey Wietharn, Norma Wilson, Cyreesa Windsor, and Kay Wolfe.

And, always, thank you to my dear customers who always show up—I am especially grateful for your support.

"In the midst of winter, I finally learned that there was in me an invincible summer."

ALBERT CAMUS